AMELIA EARHART

First Lady of Flight
by Jan Parr

A Book Report Biography
FRANKLIN WATTS
A Division of Grolier Publishing
New York / London / Hong Kong / Sydney
Danbury, Connecticut

The publisher would like to thank Loretta Jean Gragg,
Executive Director of the Ninety-Nines, Inc., for her expertise and
assistance in the preparation of this book.

Cover illustration by Natalie Ascencios

Photographs ©: Art Resource: 39 (Bridgeman Art Library),
14, 22, 23, 38 (Giraudon); Corbis-Bettmann: 8, 9, 10, 36, 53, 56;
Gamma-Liaison: 51 (Isabel Cutler); Library of Congress: 3, 26;
North Wind Picture Archives: 6, 31, 41; Photo Researchers: 28;
Reproduced by courtesy of the Trustees, The National Gallery, London:
48; Seaver Center for Western History Research, Natural History Museum of Los Angeles County: 2; Superstock, Inc. 34, 35 (Christie's, London),
25 (Collection of the Duke of Berwick & Alba, Madrid), 19, 30, 33, 55
(National Portrait Gallery, London), 43, 45; Topham Picturepoint: 12, 17, 21.

Parr, Jan.
    Amelia Earhart: First Lady of Flight / Jan Parr.
        p. cm.—(A book report biography)
    Includes bibliographical references and index.
    Summary: Examines the life and disappearance of the pilot who was
the first woman to cross the Atlantic in a plane by herself.
    ISBN 0-531-11407-4
    1. Earhart, Amelia, 1897–1937—Juvenile literature. 2. Women air
pilots—United States—Biography—Juvenile literature. [1. Earhart,
Amelia, 1897–1937. 2. Air pilots. 3. Women—Biography.] I. Title. II. Series.
    TL540.E3P37   1997
    629.13'092—dc21   97-8156
    [B]   CIP   AC

CONTENTS

INTRODUCTION
7

CHAPTER ONE
GROWING UP AMELIA
11

CHAPTER TWO
DISCOVERING HERSELF, AND FLYING
22

CHAPTER THREE
THE *FRIENDSHIP* FLIGHT
35

CHAPTER FOUR
MARRIAGE
49

CHAPTER FIVE
HIGH FLIER
59

CHAPTER SIX
LAST FLIGHT
75

CHAPTER SEVEN
WHAT HAPPENED TO AMELIA EARHART?
89

CHRONOLOGY
101

MAJOR AVIATION RECORDS
103

SOURCES
105

FOR MORE INFORMATION
107

INTERNET RESOURCES
108

INDEX
109

It had been twenty hours since Amelia Earhart and her navigator, Fred Noonan, left Lae, New Guinea. It was July of 1937, and the world's most famous female pilot was attempting to set yet another in a string of records she had already set or broken: she was trying to be the first person to fly around the world at the equator. She had already flown 22,000 miles (35,400 km). This was the final stretch: only 7,000 miles (11,300 km) to go. They were headed for the tiny island of Howland, where they would rest and refuel for the trip back to the United States.

The two were flying a twin-engine Lockheed Electra. Amelia, in the cockpit, could not move, stand, or stretch in the space, which was just four and one-half feet square (1.4 m)—about the size of a doghouse. She had been awake for twenty-four hours. The engine noise was loud and never let up. The metal of the plane shook constantly, even more than usual now because the plane was low on fuel.

For hours, a ship called the *Itasca,* which had been sent out to keep in contact with Amelia's plane, had tried to send signals and messages to the plane and to get its position. Amelia kept changing the radio frequency and never stayed on the radio long enough for them to figure out where her plane was. The ship's crew was getting more and more worried. Then, at 8:47 A.M. on July 2, they heard Amelia's voice, hurried and upset: "KHAQQ to *Itasca.* We are on the line of position one five seven dash three three seven. Will repeat this message on 6210 kilocycles. . . . We are running north and south."

It was the last message they would hear.

A huge search party of planes and boats came up empty. No trace of Amelia's plane, or of Amelia or Fred Noonan, was found.

THE FATE OF A PIONEER

The question of what happened has fascinated people for the sixty years since Amelia made her last, fateful flight. But even if she had not disappeared, Amelia Earhart would still have been remembered as an important figure in aviation history as well as one of the world's great feminists, a role model for other women who wanted to accomplish things that no one had done before.

She accomplished these great achievements in the 1920s and 1930s. It was a time when women were not supposed to wear pants, much less pilot a plane. But Amelia was a pioneer.

She found she had instantly become famous

Amelia Earhart is remembered as a pioneer in aviation and in advancing the role of women in society.

in 1928 when she was the first woman passenger to cross the Atlantic Ocean in a plane. Later, she would set many records flying planes on her own, including becoming the first woman to pilot a plane across the Atlantic. She was also a visionary: she saw, before many others did, the enormous potential of commercial airlines, the very planes we take today to go on vacation or visit relatives.

She was also a speaker and writer who spread the message that women should have equal rights. As a counselor of women students at Purdue University in Indiana, she told women that getting married was not the only path for them to choose. This was a radical idea in those days.

Whatever happened to Amelia that day in 1937, she remains one of the twentieth century's most important figures. Over the years, dozens of researchers, journalists, archaeologists, and aviation buffs have tried to solve the mystery of her disappearance. Maybe the question will never be answered. But her legacy lives on.

CHAPTER ONE

GROWING UP AMELIA

Amy Otis was twenty years old in the summer of 1890. She had dropped out of Vassar College after becoming ill. She recovered and was traveling with her father on business. One day, she joined a group climbing Pike's Peak in Colorado. About a quarter mile from the top, several members of the group got nosebleeds and had to turn back. Amy went on and became the first woman to reach the top of Pike's Peak.

Little could she know that soon she would have a daughter who would grow up to be a woman of many such firsts.

THE OTISES

Amelia Earhart was born to Amy and her husband, Edwin Earhart, in Amy's parents' home in Atchison, Kansas, on July 24, 1897. This was the first of five homes she would live in before graduating from high school in 1915.

Amelia's mother had come to the big brick-and-clapboard house to rest while she was pregnant. Amy's parents, the Otises, were distinguished members of society. Amelia's grandfather, Judge Alfred Gideon Otis, was a retired judge and president of the Atchison Savings Bank. A few days after Amelia was baptized, they returned home to Kansas City, 22 miles (35 km) south of Atchison.

But Amelia and her sister, Muriel, born two and a half years after Amelia, spent much of their childhood at the Otis home in Atchison. The house stood on a bluff high above the Missouri River. It had a big front porch shaded by old trees and was surrounded by a large lawn and trimmed shrubbery.

The house had eleven rooms and was often filled with prominent men of the town, discussing politics and business while sitting in overstuffed chairs. China and crystal filled the dining room. On holidays, maids served food prepared by a paid cook.

In short, the Otises had money. When Amy Otis was a young woman, they expected their daughter to live much the same way they did.

Imagine, then, how they felt when she announced that she wanted to marry Edwin Earhart. Edwin was raised poor, the son of an

Evangelical Lutheran minister who did odd jobs to support his family. Edwin put himself through law school at the University of Kansas by shining shoes, building furnace fires, and tutoring other students. Edwin and Amy met at her sixteenth birthday party.

Amy's father said they could not get married until Edwin had earned at least fifty dollars a month for six months in a row. That was quite a bit of money in those days. When Edwin could do that, Mr. Otis would provide them with a furnished house in Kansas City. Five years later, Edwin made the goal: he was earning the money working in the claims department of the Rock Island Railroad's office in Kansas City. The two were married.

There were no maids, cooks, or servants in the Earhart house. Living without them was a big shock to Amy. She was also lonely, being used to a big, bustling house filled with staff and visitors. So she often went with her husband on business trips. She continued traveling even after the girls were born, so they spent a lot of time with their grandparents.

Amelia went to school at the college prep school her mother had attended in Atchison, living with her grandparents during the term. She admitted that she was a handful for her grandparents. She was a classic tomboy. Her grand-

Amelia, age six

mother worried when Amelia leaped over the fence that surrounded their tidy yard on her way to and from school. The girls asked for footballs for Christmas, and they shot rats in their grandparents' barn with a .22-caliber rifle.

"My sister and I had the first gymnasium suits in town," Amelia wrote in a book about her life. "We wore them Saturdays to play in, and though we felt terribly 'free and athletic,' we also felt somewhat as outcasts among the little girls who fluttered about us in their skirts."

Amelia never saw any reason not to do things boys did. Girls were supposed to sit up on sleds; boys were allowed to lie flat. Amelia, of course, ignored what she was "supposed" to do; on one occasion, it was a good thing she did! As Amelia wrote:

I was zipping down one of the really steep hills in town when a junk man's cart, pulled by a horse with enormous blinders, came out from a side road. The hill was so icy that I couldn't turn and the junk man didn't hear the squeals of warning. In a second my sled had slipped between the front and back legs of the horse and got clear before either he or I knew what had happened. Had I been sitting up, either my head or the horse's ribs would have suffered in contact.

But as much as Muriel and Amelia liked to sled, play sports, and spend time outside, they had another love—books. She and Muriel were good readers before they were five years old, and Amelia liked adventure stories. They loved books so much that when they had to do chores around the house, instead of working at the same time, one read aloud while the other cleaned.

Black Beauty by Anna Sewell was one of their favorites. The girls loved horses. When delivery horses came to the house, they climbed on them. A friend's father let them ride the horse that drew his wagon. The two girls became especially attached to the neighbor's mare, a horse that was treated cruelly. Amelia never forgave the neighbor when the mare bolted one day to escape being whipped, fell off a bridge, and died. When Amelia's mother asked her to take a piece of cake to the neighbor (he had been slightly hurt chasing the mare), she refused.

Meanwhile, Edwin Earhart had begun drinking heavily. The disapproving gaze of his wife's parents was never far away. He began to do poorly at his job at the railroad office because of his drinking, and life at home was not always peaceful. Finally, he lost his job.

He began looking for other work immediately, but Kansas City was a small town; everyone knew his reputation as an alcoholic. He started looking

*A family portrait of the Otises and Earharts;
Amelia (center) and her sister, Muriel (left),
were very independent children.*

for jobs in other cities, finally finding one in the
claims department of the Rock Island Railroad in
Des Moines, Iowa. Amy moved with him, but
Muriel and Amelia, who was nine at the time,
stayed with their grandparents in Atchison.

When school ended, the girls joined their parents. Des Moines was very different from Kansas City, where they had been known as the judge's granddaughters. But they made new friends and learned to adapt. In 1908, at age eleven, Amelia saw her first airplane at the Iowa State Fair. At that time, these "flying machines" were rare and unusual. (Orville and Wilbur Wright had only made their first flight in December 1903.) But Amelia, who had only seen airplanes in magazines, was not impressed with the plane. "It was a thing of rusty wire and wood and not at all interesting," she later recalled.

"It was a thing of rusty wire and wood and not at all interesting."

They did not stay in Iowa very long. Edwin, still unable to control his drinking, was fired again. He once again looked for a new job, but this time could find only a minor law clerk's position in Saint Paul, Minnesota. Again, the family prepared to move.

THE GIRL IN BROWN WHO WALKS ALONE

By this time, Amelia was becoming expert at dealing with change and new situations. She grew to be very independent and helped her mother, who was used to having servants, run the household. Amelia always got good grades and continued to enjoy reading. She also played on the basketball team.

Her father's drinking, however, bothered her. One day she found a bottle of whiskey in his suitcase as he was packing for a business trip. She emptied the bottle into the sink; as she was doing so, her father saw her. He raised his arm to hit her, but her mother stopped him. Although he said he was sorry, the incident stayed with Amelia.

A few months later, he was drinking again. He came home three hours late one day, even though he had promised to escort Amelia and Muriel to a school dance that night. Amelia was very disappointed.

To add to Edwin's problems, he was stinging from a deliberate slight in Amy's mother's will. Mrs. Otis died in 1911, leaving about a million dollars—a lot of money now but even more back then. She left it to be divided among Amy and her three siblings. But Amy's share was put in a trust that could not be touched for twenty years, or until Edwin's death. The Otises, it seemed, never trusted their son-in-law and wanted to protect Amy and her daughters so that they would have money in later years. They were afraid he would drink it away or lose it another way.

From Saint Paul, the family moved to Springfield, Missouri, where Edwin had been promised a job with the Chicago, Burlington, and Quincy Railroad. But when they got there, he found out that a mistake had been made. There was no job.

At this point, Amy Earhart had had enough moving around. Such a life was not good for the girls, she said, so the three of them moved to Chicago, into the home of close friends, the Shedds. Amy planned that they would join Edwin once he established a law office in Kansas City. After a year of living with the Shedds, who treated them like family, Amy and her daughters moved to a small apartment in Hyde Park, on the south side of Chicago.

Amelia was fifteen and an excellent student when she entered high school. There she became known as a loner who fought for unpopular causes. An English teacher in the school was nearly deaf, and the children made fun of her. Amelia felt bad for the teacher, but she also thought it was a waste of time to sit in the class. She lobbied to have the teacher removed. It was said that such teachers were on the payroll because they had "connections" with city hall. None of her classmates joined her in this cause, however, and it made her more of an outsider than ever. Eventually, Amelia got permission to read on her own in the school library during the English class.

Amelia did not attend her graduation. In the school yearbook, she was described as "The girl in brown who walks alone."

After Amelia graduated, she went with her mother and sister to Kansas City to join Edwin. He had stopped drinking and had his own law practice. But things would never be the same. The years of drinking and moving from place to place had taken their toll. Amelia would never really live with the family again. Edwin pressured his wife to break her mother's will, only to find that there was less money than they thought because Amy's brother had not managed the trust very well. There was only $60,000 left for Amy's share instead of the $250,000 she was expecting. But it was enough to send the girls to prep school to get them ready for college.

CHAPTER TWO

DISCOVERING HERSELF, AND FLYING

Amelia enrolled in Ogontz School, a prep school near Philadelphia, Pennsylvania, with an eye toward going on to Bryn Mawr College, also near Philadelphia, a school she had dreamed of attending for years.

As always, Amelia took a leadership role at the school and did not hesitate to speak up when she felt things were wrong. She belonged to several "secret societies" at the school but was dismayed to find that some girls were excluded. She asked the school's headmistress to allow the creation of a new secret society so that all the girls could belong to a group. She was painfully aware of what it felt like to be an outsider. (When Amelia was a senior, the headmistress banned secret societies altogether.)

She also spoke out about the school's policy of

not allowing the young women to study women's rights. This and some other subjects were considered "unsuitable" for girls. Amelia believed that all books should be available for study. But she could not find books at school on all the subjects that interested her.

WORLD WAR I

Such were the times she lived in. Young women were supposed to know their place—that is, at home, rather than out in the world. But in 1917, when the United States entered World War I, all that changed. Since most American men had left to fight in Europe, women were needed to fill in for all sorts of traditionally male positions: nurses, mechanics, ambulance drivers, and more. Amelia started a scrapbook filled with articles about women who had made careers for themselves. These women had jobs that had once been held only by men: a fire lookout, a bricklayer, a bank president, a president of a medical association, a worker in the federal forestry service.

Also in her scrapbook was an article about legislation on the state level to remove discrimination against women with regard to property rights and to grant rights of inheritance. Amelia wrote next to the article: "This method is not sound. Women will gain economic justice by providing for themselves in all lines of endeavor, not by having laws passed for them."

Amelia was becoming a leader herself: she was voted vice president of the class and secretary to the local Red Cross chapter. Some students fought to have sororities come back, but Amelia opposed them. She also asked that instead of buying an expensive class ring, seniors buy a cheaper one and give the extra money to the Red Cross. Needless to say, her positions were not always popular.

Then, over the Christmas holidays, Amelia visited her sister in Toronto. Muriel was in prep school there, getting ready to attend Smith College. Though Amelia had been involved with the Red Cross and had done some knitting for soldiers overseas, she had little firsthand knowledge, until that visit, of the Great War, as World War I was called. In Toronto, many of Canada's young soldiers, who had been in the war from the beginning, were returning wounded to a local military hospital.

"I can't bear the thought of going back to school and being useless."

Amelia later wrote: "One day I saw four one-legged men at once, walking as best they could down the street together." She told her mother, "I'd like to stay here and help in the hospitals. I can't bear the thought of going back to school and being useless."

After the New Year, she returned to Ogontz. A few weeks later, though, she rejoined her sister in

Amelia as a volunteer nurse in Toronto, 1917

Toronto, where she took a Red Cross course to become a nurse's aide. She abandoned all plans of a college degree.

As a nurse's aide at a military hospital, Amelia scrubbed floors, played tennis with the patients, served meals, massaged cramps, and pitched in wherever she could. On her days off, she met Muriel to ride horses or visited former patients at local airfields.

When she had first seen an airplane back in Des Moines, she was not impressed. This time, though, the flying machines at the airfields caught her interest. She wrote:

> Though I had seen one or two of them at county fairs before, I now saw many of them. . . . Of course, no civilian had opportunity of going up. But I hung around in my spare time and absorbed all I could. I remember the sting of snow on my face as it was blown back from the propellers when the training planes took off on skis.

When a great flu epidemic broke out, Amelia worked around the clock at the military hospital until she, too, caught the flu. The war ended while she was ill.

Her flu turned into pneumonia. She went to Northampton, Massachusetts, where her sister was at Smith College, and later to Lake George, in upstate New York, to rest. While in Northampton, Amelia took a course in car-engine repair for women. She learned basic mechanical skills in the class, abilities that would come in handy later when she became an airline pilot. At this point, however, Amelia was convinced that she wanted to study medicine. So when she became healthy again, she moved to New York City to attend Columbia University.

While at Columbia, Amelia enjoyed everything the big city had to offer. Once, she talked a custodian into giving her the key to a trapdoor that opened onto a spiral staircase leading to the dome of Columbia's library. From the narrow walkway at the base of the dome, Amelia and a girlfriend could see all of New York stretched out before them. As they sat looking at the city, Amelia's friend told her that someone had proposed to her. "I can think of lots of things worse than never getting married," Amelia said. "And one of the worst is being married to a man who tied you down. I'm not sold on marriage at all for myself, but of course, I'm not in love with anybody—yet."

"I can think of lots of things worse than never getting married."

Within a few months, Amelia decided she was not cut out to be a doctor. She thought perhaps she would work in medical research. At the same time, her mother and father, who were then living in California and trying to keep their marriage together, asked Amelia to come live with them. Since it did not seem that she was serious about school, it appeared to be the perfect solution. Amelia, however, resented that she had to go to California while her sister, whom she called Pidge, stayed at Smith. Before she left, she told Muriel, "I'll see what I can do to keep Mother and Dad together, Pidge, but after that I'm going to come back here and live my own life."

Amelia was twenty-three. She was tall and slim, with long hair, big eyes, and a boyish grin. She was not pretty in the usual way, but she was quite attractive. She had not had a serious boyfriend, and she had no real idea what she wanted to do in life.

LEARNING TO FLY

Both things changed when Amelia got to California. Her mother had rejoined her father in Los Angeles. He had stopped drinking and had a good law practice. They lived in a large house, much larger than they needed. So they rented out the extra rooms to three boarders, one of them a chemical engineer named Sam Chapman. Sam was a good-looking, educated man about Amelia's age. Amelia was immediately attracted to him, and he to her.

Sam and Amelia went to plays together, swam, and played tennis. They had a lot in common. Together they also attended illegal meetings of a socialist workers' group called the Industrial Workers of the World. At least one of the meetings they attended was broken up by the police. But it was not like Amelia to be afraid of authority. It looked as though Sam and Amelia were made for one another. Amelia, however, had other ideas.

At an air show on Long Beach, she rekindled the interest in flying she had first discovered in Toronto. She asked her father how much it would cost to take flying lessons. He found out that it cost about a thousand dollars to learn to fly. "Why do you want to know?" he asked her. He booked her a flight for the next day. "I am sure he thought that one ride would be enough for me," she later wrote.

The next day, in a suburb of Los Angeles, her father paid the ten-dollar fee for Amelia to be a passenger on a ten-minute flight. "As soon as we left the ground, I knew I myself had to fly," Amelia wrote. "Miles away I saw the ocean and the Hollywood hills seemed to peep over the edge of the cockpit, as if they were already friends." Finally she had found her calling:

"'I think I'd like to fly,' I told the family casually that evening, knowing full well I'd die if I didn't. 'Not a bad idea,' said my father, equally casually. 'When do you start?'"

"'I think I'd like to fly,' I told the family casually that evening, knowing full well I'd die if I didn't."

Clearly her father did not take her seriously. Her mother did not object, so Amelia said she would look into flying lessons. Before long, she had signed up for twelve hours of lessons and expected her parents to pay the fee of five hundred dollars. Edwin told her he could not afford it. Amelia was determined to get her way, so she said she would get a job and pay for them herself. She began working in her father's office.

Edwin objected to his daughter spending unsupervised time alone with a male flight instructor. But Amelia had an answer for that, too: she found a female pilot who gave lessons, Anita "Neta" Snook. Neta was one of the first female pilots. She gave lessons and took curious people on rides in her plane, a Curtiss Canuck.

Neta was just a year older than Amelia but had been flying for years. She recalled the day that Edwin and Amelia arrived at the small airfield. "She was wearing a brown suit, plain but of good cut. Her hair was braided and neatly coiled around her head; there was a light scarf around

"Neta" Snook (left) gave Amelia her first flying lessons in her Curtiss Canuck biplane.

her neck and she carried gloves. She would have stood out in any crowd. . . . 'I'm Amelia Earhart and this is my father. . . . I want to learn to fly and I understand you teach students. . . . Will you teach me?'"

Amelia took to Neta immediately. She wrote to her sister: "I want you to meet my instructor. . . . She dresses and talks like a man and can do everything around a plane that a man can do. I'm lucky that she'll teach me, not only because she will give me lessons on credit, but because she is a top-notch flier."

For her first lesson, Amelia wore old brown riding breeches and a tailored brown jacket. She learned to taxi the plane, that is, drive it on the ground. She also began reading a book on aerodynamics—the laws of objects flying through the air—that she had borrowed from the library. It would be several weeks before she would take a plane up in the air. Amelia had taken a job working in the mailroom of the telephone company offices in addition to working a half day on Saturdays at her father's office. The mailroom position was her first real job.

Neta and Amelia became friends. They often went out on double dates; Amelia was still dating Sam Chapman. One day, Amelia told Neta that she had secretly been cutting her hair off an inch or so every few weeks. Long hair was impractical for a pilot, she believed. She had kept it coiled on her head when she was at home, afraid her mother would disapprove. Within a few months, though, it was as short as a boy's.

After six months of lessons, Neta did not think Amelia was a very good pilot. She discouraged her from trying to buy a plane, something Amelia wanted very much. She thought Amelia was distracted and not careful enough. During one flight, Amelia failed to check the fuel gauge, even when Neta asked her about it beforehand. It could have been a fatal mistake.

Amelia believed in herself, however, and set herself a goal of buying a Kinner Airster airplane, a lightweight plane with an air-cooled engine. Just before she turned twenty-five, she paid $2,000 for a bright yellow plane she called the *Canary*. To scrape together the money, she borrowed all of her sister's savings and got the rest from her mother. In return, her mother asked that she give up the mailroom job at the telephone company. She did, but she stayed on as a telephone operator.

Amelia still had not flown solo. She continued her lessons with Neta in the *Canary*, which was smaller than Neta's Curtiss Canuck and harder to handle. Then one day, not long after getting the *Canary*, Amelia had her first crash.

She was flying with Neta to look at the first aircraft made by airplane designer Donald Douglas (who went on to run the huge aircraft company now called McDonnell Douglas). The *Canary* was not going up fast enough to clear some trees, so Amelia did the only thing she could—she pulled the nose of the plane up, which caused it to stall and crash. No one was hurt, but the propeller broke and the landing gear was damaged. The women climbed out, and Amelia began powdering her nose. Even at this age, she knew that appearances were important. "We have to look nice when the reporters come," she told Neta.

> **"We have to look nice when the reporters come."**

A former World War I pilot named John "Monte" Montijo gave Amelia more advanced lessons. Finally, she was ready to fly solo. Her first solo flight did not go as well as she would have liked. On takeoff, a shock absorber broke, causing a wing to sag. Instead of coming right back down, however, Amelia took the plane up to 5,000 feet (1,520 m) and flew for a while before making a bad landing. Neta and Monte were upset. Nonetheless, Amelia celebrated her first solo flight by buying a leather flying coat. She wanted the coat to look broken in, so she walked on it and even slept in it. Image counted, Amelia believed.

CHAPTER THREE

THE FRIENDSHIP FLIGHT

Neta Snook sold her airplane and left Los Angeles in 1921. Amelia stayed on at the airstrip. In the summer of 1922, Amelia was pictured in the *Los Angeles Examiner* with her airplane, the *Canary*. In the accompanying interview, she said she hoped to fly across the continent the following year. She added that she thought of "dropping in at Vassar College" to take a course. "I don't crave publicity," she said, "but it seems to me it would be the greatest fun."

Amelia flew as much as she could, continuing to work at various part-time jobs to earn money for fuel. Then in October of 1922, she handed her father and Muriel two tickets to an air show in Los Angeles. "I won't be able to sit with you," Muriel recalls her saying. Amelia disappeared once they got to the field. Then the announcer of the air show said that a young lady was going to try to set an altitude record in a Kinner biplane. It was then that her father and Muriel saw Amelia climbing into the air in her plane. Watching the little yellow aircraft in the sky, "both of us were desperately worried," Muriel said. Amelia set an altitude record for women by flying to 14,000 feet (4,270 m). She held the record for only a few weeks, when another woman pilot, Ruth Nichols, flew higher.

Amelia then attempted to regain the record but failed. She would not get another chance for a while because she was forced to sell the *Canary* to get cash. Her mother's inheritance had been wiped out in an investment Amelia had encouraged. The money was invested in a gypsum mine (gypsum is a type of mineral) in California run by a friend of Amelia's. A flash flood wiped out the mine and, with it, Amy's money. Amelia sold her plane to help buy a truck for the mining operation. She worked part-time helping to run the trucking company. Sometimes she even drove the truck.

About this time, Sam Chapman became interested in marrying Amelia. Several other men were interested in her as well. But Amelia did not seem serious about marriage to Sam or anyone else.

The year 1924 was not the best for Amelia and her family. Amelia suffered from very painful sinus problems; they became so bad that she had to have surgery. In the same year, her mother and father filed for divorce. Amelia did manage to buy another Kinner plane, but she did not love it as she had loved the *Canary*.

BACK EAST

Muriel, Amelia, and their mother decided to move back east to Massachusetts. Muriel went by train to start summer classes at Harvard. Amelia sold her second airplane and bought a bright yellow car called a Kissel. She and her mother got in the car and took the long way east—going north and touring national parks. Cross-country travel by car was still new in those days. Along the way, Amelia wrote, "groups gathered to ask me questions about conditions of roads, how I'd come, why I'd come, and any number of other questions."

Amelia's sinus troubles were still causing her much pain, and the doctors recommended another operation. That did the trick. After a week in the hospital, Amelia said that it was the first time she had been without pain in four years.

She returned to Columbia University but found she had no more direction as a student than she had had years ago, before going to California. What's more, the family needed money. Muriel was teaching school in a Boston suburb. Amelia found a position as a social worker at Denison

House, Boston's second-oldest settlement house. It was a place that provided help and support for Boston's immigrant families—Syrians, Irish, and Chinese. Amelia loved it. "The people whom I met through Denison House were as interesting as any I have ever known," she wrote. Eventually she moved into the house. She taught English, visited families, and performed many other duties.

Sam Chapman had followed Amelia to Boston with the idea of marrying her. He was hurt when she moved into Denison House. Amelia repeatedly turned down his proposals of marriage. The more Sam urged her to change her mind, the more strongly she refused. Sam was an old-fashioned man who believed husbands should support their wives and children. He worried that she disapproved of the hours he kept as an engineer, so he told her he would quit and get any job she wanted him to.

This offer only made her more upset. She told her sister, "I don't want to tell Sam what he should do. He ought to *know* what makes him happiest, and then do it, no matter what other people say. I know what I want to do, and I expect to do it, married or single!"

What she wanted to do was fly.

Amelia got to know local pilots. She became vice president of the local chapter of the National Aeronautic Association. She flew a few times. She also became a minor investor and director in a company that would build a local airport. Her name started appearing in the Boston newspapers, and she was beginning to be known as a pilot and as someone who wanted to further women's accomplishments in aviation.

She watched with intense interest as Charles Lindbergh prepared for his May 1927 flight across the Atlantic Ocean—the first person to make the journey by himself. Lindbergh, who was just twenty-five, would fly the *Spirit of St. Louis*. He crossed from Long Island, New York, to Paris in thirty-three hours and thirty minutes. They young pilot was hailed as a hero.

Not long after Lindbergh's flight, Amelia received a phone call that would change her life forever.

She was busy organizing the children after school at Denison House when she was told she had a call. "I'm too busy to answer just now," she said. "Ask whoever is calling to try again later." But the caller said it was very important. "Very unwillingly I went to the telephone to hear a pleasant masculine voice say, 'Hello. You don't know me, but my name is Railey—Captain H. H. Railey.'" He asked if she would be interested in doing some flying. He added that it could be dangerous but would not say more on the phone. She asked for personal references so she could confirm that he was who he said he was. Then she agreed to meet him at his office later that evening.

Railey, it turns out, had been given the job of finding just the right female pilot to make the first flight across the Atlantic—with a male crew. The flight would be sponsored by Mrs. Frederick Guest. Amy Phipps Guest was an American who had married the Right Honorable Frederick Guest of London. She had bought a Fokker F7 airplane from Admiral Richard Byrd. She named it the *Friendship,* to represent relations between the United States and England. Amy wanted to be the first woman to fly the Atlantic, but her family talked her out of it.

Railey knew almost immediately that Amelia was the one. He was struck by how much she looked like Charles Lindbergh. Amelia was attractive, educated, well-mannered, and, of course, a pilot. She was the perfect woman for a flight that would attract worldwide attention. "I might as well lay the cards on the table," he said. "Would you fly the Atlantic?"

A week later she went to New York to meet several of the flight's backers. Amelia learned more about the flight, to be done in the *Friendship.* She met George Palmer Putnam, who had been hired to arrange and publicize the flight. She and George hit it off during her short visit, but she recalled later that he had kept her waiting in his office and did not offer to pay her train fare back to Boston. The meeting was the start of a relationship between the two that would always be part professional, part personal.

CAPTAIN OF THE *FRIENDSHIP*

Two days after her trip to New York, she got a note saying she had been chosen to be captain of the flight. She had to sign a contract that said she would not receive any money for the flight. The pilot would receive $20,000 and the mechanic $5,000, a lot of money in those days.

Amelia also had to agree not to talk about the flight. The sponsors feared that if word got out, other pilots would attempt the same route before the *Friendship* took off. Her employer, Marion Perkins, and Sam Chapman, who had remained Amelia's friend even after she had turned down his marriage proposal, were the only ones she told. Even her family was kept in the dark.

Though she would not be at the controls, Amelia was to be in charge of the flight, having final say on any matter that came up. Amelia said that if the weather was clear, she wanted to take a turn at the controls. She had no experience flying a plane with more than one engine and had never used instruments to fly, so it was unlikely that she would get the opportunity.

Amelia knew how dangerous this trip was. Women had tried to cross the Atlantic Ocean at least four other times. Each time, the women and their male flight crews died. Amelia wrote notes to her family, to be opened in the event of her death.

To her father she wrote:

May 20, 1928

Dearest Dad,

Hooray for the last grand adventure! I wish I had won but it was worth while anyway. You know that. . . .

To her mother:

Even though I have lost, the adventure was worth while. Our family tends to be too secure. My life has really been very happy, and I don't mind contemplating its end in the midst of it. . . .

The crew waited for the weather to be just right. Early on the morning of June 4, 1928, they prepared to take off. As soon as the *Friendship* lifted off, Boston newspaper reporters began calling Amy and Muriel. Sam Chapman had promised to tell Amelia's sister and mother about the flight, but he was not as fast as the reporters.

The next day, the *Friendship* landed in Halifax, Newfoundland. Amelia sent her mother a cable: "Know you will understand why I could not tell plans of flight. Don't worry. No matter what happens it will have been worth the trying. Love, A." Her mother's answer: "We are not worrying. Wish I were with you. Good luck and cheerio. Love, Mother."

The three could not take off again the next

Amelia in the Friendship, *the plane that took her across the Atlantic in 1928*

day because of heavy fog. They waited for two long weeks. During the wait, they looked through their cargo and threw out anything that might weigh down the plane. Amelia's baggage consisted only of a toothbrush, a small packet of food (the crew ate scrambled-egg sandwiches, oranges, and chocolate, washed down with coffee), notes from Americans to friends in England, and a book, *Skyward*, written by Admiral Byrd, who had sold the plane to Mrs. Guest. The book was to be given to Mrs. Guest when they arrived in England.

"We are not worrying. Wish I were with you. Good luck and cheerio. Love, Mother."

They took off from Halifax on the morning of June 17, 1928. Amelia's job was to keep the plane's log, but there was also time to look at the beautiful scenery out the window. When it got cold up in the clouds, she put on a fur-lined flight suit. She was sorry she was not permitted to fly. "The idea of going as just 'extra weight' did not appeal to me at all," she wrote.

Many hours into the flight, the crew became worried: with just an hour's worth of fuel left, they still did not see land. About an hour earlier, they had spotted a ship. They tried to make contact in order to learn their location, but their radio equipment was not working. The crew hoped the ship would paint some directions on its deck, but it did not. In desperation, Amelia attached a note to a couple of oranges and threw it down. It missed the ship.

Amelia noted in her log that they flew on in the rain, surrounded by fog. Suddenly some factory chimneys came into sight. They landed the plane in a small bay. In the log, Amelia left the location blank.

No one seemed to pay attention to them. Some men who were working on the railroad stopped to look at the plane, then turned their backs and continued their work! It was an hour before a small boat reached them and brought the tired, cold crew to shore. They were not in Ireland, as they had thought, but a small town called Burry Port, Wales. It was far from Southampton, England, where they had originally planned to land.

By the time the crew reached shore, word had spread throughout the village, and some two hundred people were waiting to greet them. They tore at their clothes and made an enormous fuss over Amelia, the first woman to fly in a plane across the Atlantic. The press called her "Lady Lindy," a nickname George Putnam had given her because she looked so much like Charles Lindbergh.

The attention embarrassed Amelia. After all, she had not done even a minute of actual flying! "The credit belongs to [the crew] and to the flight's

Bill Stultz, Amelia, and Lou Gordon, the Friendship
*crew, parading through the streets of New York City
after their transatlantic flight.*

backer as well as to the manufacturers of the plane and motors," she said. She responded to a congratulatory telegram from President Calvin Coolidge by giving credit to Bill Stultz, the pilot.

Nevertheless, Amelia was a new celebrity. She spent two weeks in London giving speeches and going to parties, teas, sports tournaments, and plays. Then the crew boarded a steamship and sailed home. In New York, Boston, and Chicago they were greeted by cheering crowds and took part in parades. Then Amelia settled down to write a book called *20 hrs. 40 min.* She took the title from her final log entry, which gave the time of the transatlantic flight. While writing, she stayed in Rye, New York, at the home of George Putnam, with his wife and two children. George's secretary helped Amelia with her writing.

Amelia had bought a small sport plane while she was in England, and it arrived just as she was finishing her book. She still did not know if she would go back to social work or devote herself to flying.

It did not take long for her to figure out that she would not return to Denison House. George Putnam arranged publicity appearances for her, including lectures that she gave about the future of air travel. *Cosmopolitan* magazine made her an editor, and she wrote several articles about aviation. She modeled and designed clothes and lent

Amelia modeled clothes for fashion magazines after achieving fame for her flight across the Atlantic.

her name to the promotion of many products. These activities gave her enough money to live comfortably. Though she served on the board of directors of Denison House, Amelia's life as a social worker was over. She was a full-fledged celebrity pilot.

CHAPTER FOUR

George Putnam was good at his job. He knew how to get publicity for his clients, especially Amelia. He made the press fall in love with her. As they worked closely together, George began to fall for Amelia himself. She was a tall, slim, attractive, and independent woman. George's marriage to his first wife, Dorothy, had been in trouble for a long time. In 1930, two years after the *Friendship* flight, Dorothy moved to Florida with her two children and filed for divorce. After the divorce, George tried to convince Amelia to marry him.

It would not be easy. Amelia never had marriage as a goal. She had already turned down Sam Chapman and discouraged others.

George and Amelia were alike in some ways. Both had been avid readers of adventure books when they were children. George had a great appreciation of the American West and enjoyed

George Putnam promoted Amelia's career as a pilot and celebrity. He remained her partner in life and business as she took on more adventures. This photo shows the couple in an airplane hangar in 1937 preparing for Amelia's attempt to fly around the world.

spending time in the wilderness. He loved adventure. He had explored Greenland for New York's American Museum of Natural History. Like Amelia, he was from a well-bred family with money; he was the grandson of one of the publishing world's giants, George Putnam Sr., founder of G. P. Putnam and Sons. Amelia and George loved music, the theater, and art. Both had endless energy and enthusiasm for life.

On the other hand, George was ten years older than Amelia, who was now in her thirties. Amelia's mother did not care for him. And there was Amelia's reluctance to be tied down.

George says he proposed to Amelia at least six times between 1930 and 1931. She said no the first five times. In some of the marriages she saw around her, one or both people had to give up their dreams. Amelia had no intention of giving up her dreams. She wanted to fly and to encourage other women to get involved with aviation.

George understood Amelia's feelings, and he tried to convince her that their marriage would be different. Finally one day, when she was getting ready to take off on a flight, George asked her again. This time she nodded her head, patted his hand, and took off.

MARRIAGE TO G. P.

The Amelia Earhart/George Putnam marriage could have been the wedding of the decade. Amelia was one of America's best-known women. George had many famous and wealthy friends. But bride and groom wanted a quiet ceremony. It was so quiet, in fact, that Amelia did not even tell her mother and sister about her engagement. (In 1930, Amelia's father died after a long illness. Amelia flew to California to be with him in his final days.)

On February 7, 1931, George and Amelia were married in George's mother's home in Noank, a small fishing village in Connecticut. George had called his mother the day before to tell her of their plans. There was no time for flowers, a cake, or other decorations. The only guests were George's mother, a judge who was a family friend, the judge's son, and an uncle of George's. Amelia wore a brown suit and brown lizard-skin shoes and nothing on her head. George borrowed a ring from his mother to slip on his bride's hand.

But before the ceremony took place, Amelia needed one more reassurance. She still saw marriage as a cage. She wanted to make sure George understood her needs. She handed him a two-page, handwritten "contract":

There are some things which should be writ before we are married—things we have talked over before—most of them.

You must know again my reluctance to marry, my feeling that I shatter thereby chances in work which means most to me. I feel the move just now as foolish as anything

I could do. I know there may be compensations, but I have no heart to look ahead.

In our life together I shall not hold you to any medieval code of faithfulness to me, nor shall I consider myself bound to you similarly. If we can be honest I think the difficulties which arise may be avoided. . . .

Please let us not interfere with the other's work or play, nor let the world see our private joys or disagreements. In this connection I may have to keep some place where I can go to be by myself now and then, for I cannot guarantee to endure at all times the confinement of even an attractive cage.

I must exact a cruel promise, and that is you will let me go in a year if we find no happiness together.

She signed it "AE."

This was a daring letter for the time. It is hard to imagine any other woman telling her future husband that he was free to see other women and asking that she be given that freedom, too. The letter makes it seem as if Amelia was not really in love with George at the time. But she did care for him enough to give marriage a try.

The two went away for the weekend for a brief honeymoon and were back at their offices on

Monday. Amelia sent her sister a cable asking her to break the news to their mother. "I am much happier than I expected I could ever be in that state," Amelia later wrote her mother. "I believe the whole thing was for the best. Of course I go on in the same way as before as far as business is concerned. I haven't changed at all and will only be busier I suppose."

Amelia kept her last name, an unusually independent act in those days but perhaps not surprising, considering her fame. Everyone knew her as Amelia Earhart. George, the smart businessman, must have seen the enormous value in that name.

THE AUTOGIRO

Meanwhile, George and Amelia searched for a new aviation record for her to set. There were a dozen or so top female pilots around this time, and they had captured many of the top flying records. George and Amelia became interested in the autogiro, a new type of aircraft that was a cross between an airplane and a helicopter. On April 8, 1931, Amelia set an altitude record in the autogiro, reaching 18,451 feet (5,624 m).

Amelia then bought the autogiro and announced that she wanted to be the first to fly in one from coast to coast. George arranged for the

Beech Nut Packing Company, makers of chewing gum, to sponsor the flight. A few weeks later, Amelia took off. She stopped in several cities along the way, ending up in Los Angeles. When she got there, she found that another pilot, a man from New York, had just made the flight in the

Amelia and her autogiro—an airplane with a helicopter-like rotor on top—were surrounded by crowds of people after her cross-country flight in 1931.

same kind of machine. George was upset that their plans had been foiled. He decided that Amelia should leave immediately so that she could be the first person to make a round-trip flight across the country in an autogiro.

Those plans went sour, however, when she crashed the machine in Abilene, Texas, at an air show. As she was taking off on a demonstration flight, a rotor (like a helicopter blade) hit a landing light and flew thirty feet (9 m). It landed in a parking lot, damaging several cars and throwing metal everywhere among the crowd. Luckily, no one was hurt. But a U.S. aviation official thought Amelia had put the crowd in danger. He gave her an official reprimand, a note that warned her to be more careful. Amelia was not happy to get the note. She insisted that she had had control of the autogiro at all times and that no one had been in danger. "I am not a careless pilot," she wrote to her mother.

A few months later, she was demonstrating an autogiro at a fair in Detroit when she crashed it on landing. George, who had not been watching, heard the noise. He ran at breakneck speed toward the plane, then caught his foot on a wire and flipped over, landing on his back. When he came to, he saw Amelia coming out of the dust, waving her hands to show she was OK. George was not so lucky. He had cracked three ribs. He issued a statement to the press blaming Amelia's crash on mechanical failure. Amelia described it as "a freak accident."

George and Amelia settled into married life, dividing their time between an apartment in New York City and George's house in Rye. The house

Amelia and George enjoyed a more down-to-earth life, including gardening, in Rye, New York.

had decorations and furniture from around the world, a big stone fireplace, and large windows that looked out on a terrace and gardens. They seemed happy and in love. She even wrote a poem to him that read, in part:

To touch your hand or see your face today
Is joy.

CHAPTER FIVE

"Women must try to do things as men have tried. When they fail, their failure must be but a challenge to others," Amelia wrote.

At breakfast one day in 1932, Amelia turned to her husband and said, "Would you *mind* if I flew the Atlantic?" The subject had come up before. Amelia wanted to cross the ocean alone this time, to prove that she was more than just a famous passenger. Since Lindbergh's flight five years earlier, no one—male or female—had flown the Atlantic solo. She would fly it in her new Lockheed Vega.

Plans for this flight were kept top secret, both so that she could change her mind at any moment and so that no other female pilot would try to break the record first. The plans were made: They would try to leave in late May, depending on the weather. Another pilot would fly the plane to

Newfoundland, and Amelia would go alone from there, aiming for the British Isles.

On the morning of May 20 (the same day Lindbergh had made his flight), the weather did not look promising. But reports from the Atlantic were good—the forecast called for several days of clear weather. Amelia rushed home to change into her flying clothes: jodhpurs (like the pants one wears to ride a horse), a silk shirt and scarf, a sweater, and a jacket.

She flew to Newfoundland with her crew, pilot Bernt Balchen and mechanic Eddie Gorski. During the flight to the city of Saint John's, Amelia slept for a couple of hours. Then the three flew to the town of Harbour Grace, where Gorski checked the plane over. She asked Balchen, "Do you think I can make it?"

"You bet," he answered.

ACROSS THE ATLANTIC ALONE

Amelia took off into the sunset. At first, everything went smoothly. Amelia liked to fly at night, and she watched the moon coming out. Then, after a few hours, the altimeter failed. This had never happened to her in all her hours of flying. It was an important instrument—without it, she did not know how high she was flying. She used a barograph instead, which was another instru-

Amelia in her Lockheed Vega, the aircraft that would take her across the Atlantic alone.

ment that could give her some idea of her climb and descent.

Then she flew into a violent storm. About an hour later, she saw a small flame coming out from a broken weld in the manifold (where the exhaust pipe attaches to the motor). It was not unusual for flames to be coming from an engine (this happens when fuel and air burn under pressure), and it did not mean that the metal would fall off or that the plane would blow up, but it still worried her. "I was indeed sorry that I had looked at the break at all because the flames appeared so much worse at night than they did in the day-time," she wrote.

"The flames appeared so much worse at night."

The manifold shook violently for hours, adding to her distress. She had other problems, including ice on her wings and a leaking reserve fuel tank that dripped gas onto her shoulder. As the hours passed and daylight dawned, the split in the manifold got bigger. She began to fear that the fumes of leaking fuel would drift back to the exhaust system and explode on contact with the flames.

She decided she must come down at the first sight of land. When she spotted land some time later, she looked around for an airfield but could not find one. She decided to land in a large pasture, among some grazing cows. Instead of cheering crowds, there was just one very surprised farmhand who watched her land. "Where am I?" she called out as she climbed out of the plane.

"In Gallagher's pasture," the man answered.

What she really wanted to know was what country she had landed in. In fact, she was in the small town of Culmore, near Londonderry in

Northern Ireland. She had flown 2,026 miles (3,260 km) in fourteen hours and fifty-four minutes.

"Have you come far?" the man asked, still unsure whether the pilot, with her short hair, was a man or a woman.

"From America," she answered.

The man took her to a cottage nearby and gave her some tea. She had only taken two cans of tomato juice with her on the journey, so she was hungry and thirsty. Eventually, a car was rounded up and she was driven to Londonderry, a bigger town a few miles down the road. The local paper got word of what she had done, and after she sent several cable messages, word spread fast.

A reporter from a New York newspaper called George, who had been extremely worried. Several hours earlier, a reporter had called to say that a plane had crashed. At first, it was thought to be Amelia's plane. Twelve minutes later, George learned that it was not Amelia's plane that had fallen. Nevertheless, he was relieved to hear that she had landed safely.

Amelia, though exhausted and hungry, must have been very happy. She had set several records: she was the first woman (and only the second person) to cross the Atlantic in a plane alone; she was the only person to have flown it twice; she had crossed it in the shortest time ever (sixteen hours and twelve minutes was the previous record); she had flown the longest nonstop flight by a woman (Ruth Nichols had flown 1,977 miles [3,182 km] nonstop). Now, Amelia could truly claim to be one of the world's greatest female pilots, perhaps the very best.

She was flown to England, and in London she was greeted by cheering crowds. After buying some clothes, she went to fancy dinners and made many public appearances. The girl from Kansas danced with the Prince of Wales. She then went on a tour of Europe. George joined her in France, and the two spent some time in Paris, Rome, and Brussels. Everywhere she went, Amelia was greeted with flowers and entertained by dignitaries.

Amelia downplayed the "courage" that so many praised her for. She told a newspaper reporter: "If it took courage I wouldn't have done it. . . . I undertook the flight for my own pleasure and in a sense to justify myself."

> **"I undertook the flight for my own pleasure and in a sense to justify myself."**

Not everyone thought Amelia was worthy of all the attention. Several articles criticizing her appeared in papers and magazines. Some thought there was no point in her feat, except to make herself famous. But this was also a time when newspapers were reporting plane crashes almost daily. Amelia's flight—and the flights of other pioneers—helped inspire confidence in this new form of transportation.

George and Amelia took a ship back to the United States. This trip gave her time to rest before meeting the adoring crowds back home. In Washington, Amelia attended a dinner at the White House with President Herbert Hoover and his wife, Lou Henry. They presented to Amelia the Special Gold Medal from the National Geographic Society—the first one given to a woman.

FAMOUS FLIER

Amelia was famous. She attended dinners or gave speeches nearly every night. She did not have much time for her mother or sister. Adding to the growing distance between them was her mother's dislike of George. She refused several invitations to visit her daughter and son-in-law at their home in Rye. In fact, the relationship between Amy and Amelia, once very close, was not good.

For years, Amelia had been giving her mother money to live on. She also gave money to Muriel and her husband, Albert. But the money from Amelia had strings attached: she often wrote in her letters to her mother and sister about clothes,

U.S. President Herbert Hoover presents Amelia with the National Geographic Society's highest award after her solo transatlantic flight. Present at the presentation are (left to right): Gilbert Grosvenor, President of the National Geographic Society; President Hoover; George Putnam; Amelia; John LaGorce, Vice-President of the National Geographic Society; and Mrs. Hoover.

asking them to buy certain outfits, hats, and shoes for themselves. She was sometimes critical of the way they looked. "About clothes. Please remember that you and Pidge attract attention as my relatives," she wrote to them. "I'd prefer you to get a few simple decent clothes, both of you. Not awful cheapies, so people who don't look below the surface won't have anything to converse about."

Amelia also criticized the way Muriel and Albert spent money. Though she was one of the country's early feminists, she believed, like her grandfather, that a man should provide for his family. At one point she wrote to her mother: "I am not working to help Albert, nor Pidge much as I care for her. . . . I do not mean to be harsh, but I know the family failing about money. . . . If there were any assurance that things were run on a businesslike basis, there might be some reason for helping."

Once, Amy planned to take Muriel's young children on vacation. Amelia thought this would be too hard on her mother and told her flatly: "I want your solemn word that you will not try to [take] the two infants with you. I shall be compelled to withhold the monthly check if you do."

Meanwhile, Amelia continued her life of flying and socializing. She broke several more flight records after the transatlantic trip. In August of 1932, she set a new speed record by flying across the United States from Los Angeles, California, to Newark, New Jersey, in nineteen hours and five minutes. The next July, she made the trip in seventeen hours and seven minutes, breaking her own record.

She and George became friends with the new U.S. president, Franklin D. Roosevelt, and his wife, Eleanor. One night, during a dinner at the White House, the two women slipped away and Amelia took Mrs. Roosevelt up in a plane so she could see how beautiful it was to fly at night.

Though she was famous, Amelia did not stop speaking her mind and standing up for causes that might be unpopular. At a conference of the Daughters of the American Revolution, a group of women whose relatives had been in the Revolutionary War, she criticized the organization for campaigning for a weapons buildup to prepare for another war. How could they call for the United States to enter into war if they themselves were not willing to serve, she asked? The crowd gasped. They were not used to hearing a woman speak in such a way.

Amelia was a feminist, but she did not call herself one. She believed women could do anything men could do, but she did not see the sense in separate organizations for women only. Nevertheless, she was a member of the National Women's Party and the Ninety-Nines, a prestigious organization of women pilots. The Ninety-nines, named because it was thought that there were ninety-nine female pilots in the United States (in fact, more than 120 had licenses when the group was formed), said its aim was "to provide closer relationships among pilots and to unite them in any movement that may be for their benefit or for that of aviation in general." It held its first meeting in 1929; Amelia was elected president.

HAWAII AND MEXICO CITY

Amelia planned another big flight. Her popularity as a speaker would diminish if she did not continue to make dramatic flights; she could not rest on her past accomplishments. She decided to fly from Hawaii to California, over the Pacific Ocean, in her Vega airplane. Other people had flown from California to Hawaii, but no one had gone the other way. George organized the venture, finding sponsors to pay to fix up her plane, buy fuel, and cover other costs. He hired Paul Mantz, who flew as a stunt pilot in the movies, to help her plan the flight and check out her plane. Amelia was fortunate to work with such an expert.

Once again, the flight was kept secret. In December of 1934, Paul Mantz, George, and Amelia sailed for Hawaii, all the while denying that Amelia was going to fly the Pacific Ocean. Instead, she claimed she was going to give lectures and fly around the islands of Hawaii.

The newspapers, meanwhile, found out that Amelia's flight was on. Many critics came out against it. One crew, headed by Englishman Sir Charles Kingsford-Smith, had already charted the route successfully. Why was Amelia trying it, they wondered? Ten pilots had already died trying to make the crossing. Just a month before, a plane had disappeared on the same route. For forty-seven days, army and navy planes and ships searched for the crew; they were never found. Such searches were expensive and risked even more lives, the newspapers argued.

Then the U.S. Navy refused to clear Amelia's departure. They said that her radio equipment was not good enough. To prove them wrong, Paul Mantz flew up to 12,000 feet (3,650 m) and, from there, was able to radio Kingman, Arizona. The navy was satisfied. Then the crew waited for the weather to cooperate. Finally on January 11, 1935, Amelia took off, as two hundred people watched and news cameras captured the scene.

This time, unlike the flight across the Atlantic, everything went smoothly—no broken equipment or bad weather. And this time, using a two-way radio telephone, she was able to maintain contact during the flight. The radio was used to broadcast the flight nationwide through radio stations. In order for the radio to work, she had to push an antenna through a small hole in the cabin floor, then reel it back up again when she

January 18, 1935

My dear Miss Earhart:

I am pleased to send you this message of congratulations. You have scored again.

By successfully spanning the ocean stretches between Hawaii and California, following your triumphant trans-Atlantic flight of 1928, you have shown even the "doubting Thomases" that aviation is a science which cannot be limited to men only.

Because of swift advances in this science of flight, made possible by Government and private enterprise, scheduled ocean transportation by air is a distinct and definite future prospect.

The trail-blazers who opened to civilization the vast stretches of this Continent of ours, who moved our boundary from the Atlantic to the Pacific, were inspired and helped by women of courage and skill. From the days of these pioneers to the present era, women have marched step in step with men. And now, when air trails between our shores and those of our neighbors are being charted, you, as a woman, have preserved and carried forward this precious tradition.

Very sincerely yours,

Franklin D. Roosevelt

Miss Amelia Earhart,
Oakland, California.

A letter from U.S. President Franklin Delano Roosevelt congratulates Amelia on her flight from Hawaii to California. President and Mrs. Roosevelt were friends of George Putnam and Amelia and supporters of her efforts.

was done. Thousands of Americans listening on their radios at home heard Amelia talking as she flew across the ocean. She landed in Oakland, California, about eighteen hours later. Thousands of people were there to meet her. The flight was a real triumph.

Once again Amelia hit the lecture circuit. In New York, she met the consul general of Mexico. He asked her to fly to Mexico City. George sprang into action. He knew that such a flight would gain a lot of publicity. The Mexican government issued a special postage stamp to mark the flight, and George arranged to buy three hundred of the stamps so he could put them on autographed covers and sell them to collectors. He figured the money from the stamps would pay for the entire flight.

Amelia left Los Angeles on April 19, 1935, bound for Mexico City. Toward the end of the flight, she lost her way, and she landed in a dry lake bed about 50 miles (80 km) from her goal. Some peasants gave her directions, and she took off again. She landed safely in Mexico City to the welcome of the country's president. After several weeks of waiting for the weather to clear, she flew back to Newark, New Jersey. Again, she was mobbed by crowds.

She went right back to lecturing, but her exhausting schedule soon landed her in bed with another bad sinus problem. She had another sinus operation and then came down with pleurisy (a condition that includes chills, fever, and painful coughing and breathing). She was in California at the time and had to stay in bed for ten days.

Amelia loved California and its pleasant weather. She convinced George, a die-hard Easterner, to buy a house there. The decision was a bit easier since their house in Rye, New York, had been partially destroyed by a fire several months earlier. She and Paul Mantz, who lived in California, were planning to start a flying school. She must have realized that she could not continue to make record-breaking flights forever and needed a plan for the future.

In the fall of 1935, Amelia had accepted a faculty position at Purdue University in Lafayette, Indiana. She would spend a few weeks there every semester teaching and advising young women. She would also work in Purdue's aeronautics and aviation department.

Amelia greatly enjoyed her time at Purdue, where she stayed in a dormitory and ate meals with the students. Her lectures were always packed. After dinner, she would often visit with students in their rooms, sitting on the floor with them. Purdue wanted to pay Amelia back for her

*The Lockheed Electra, the plane that would take
Amelia on both her attempts to fly around the world*

contributions to the students and the university.
The Purdue Research Foundation donated about
$40,000 to buy Amelia a twin-engine plane. Up to
this point, she had flown only single-engine aircraft. The new plane was an Electra, Lockheed's
most modern design, with many instruments and
features. Amelia hoped she could carry passen-
gers and study the effects of flying on men and
women. But first, before that research, before the
flying school, she had one last flight to make.

She wanted to fly around the world.

CHAPTER SIX

LAST FLIGHT

Other people had flown around the world before, but not at the equator, its widest point. The others had usually circled near the North or South Pole. Why did Amelia want to fly around the world at its equator? For one thing, she and George realized that there were not many other aviation records left to break. For another, her past flights had always been charted by someone before her—she was the first person to go alone or the first woman or she flew the route faster. But now she would blaze her own trail. Such an accomplishment would validate her fame and secure her future as a teacher, flight instructor, writer, and lecturer.

And there was another reason. As she wrote in *Last Flight,* a book published after her disappearance, "Now and then women should do for themselves what men have already done—and occasionally what men have not done—thereby establishing themselves as persons, and perhaps encouraging other women toward greater independence of thought and action."

> **"Now and then women should do for themselves what men have already done—and occasionally what men have not done."**

Amelia got her new plane on her thirty-ninth birthday. Paul Mantz worked countless hours with Amelia, training her to fly the twin-engine plane. It was very different from her old Vega, and at times Mantz got impatient with how slowly Amelia learned the controls. He was never quite sure that she had mastered flying the Electra.

PLANNING THE TRIP

While Amelia continued to lecture, George arranged the complicated details of the flight. He wrote to their friends in the White House, the Roosevelts, to ask for help from the State Department in flying over so many different countries. He also had to find out about the conditions of runways around the world. The friendship with the president helped: clearances that might have taken weeks or months were granted in days.

George also arranged for the trip to take

place at the same time as Pan Am, the country's first commercial airline, was testing a route; Amelia could use the ships Pan Am had set up along part of the route for weather reports and emergency help. Fred Noonan, a navigator who had worked for Pan Am, signed on to fly with Amelia. Some accounts say that Noonan, who had a reputation as a heavy drinker, was let go by Pan Am because of his habit. If Amelia saw the irony in becoming involved once again with an alcoholic, as her father was, she never mentioned it. Captain Harry Manning, commander of the ship that brought Amelia home from her first Atlantic flight, would be radioman and senior navigator. Mantz would not fly with the crew; he was responsible for making sure the plane was in tip-top condition.

Amelia announced her plans to the press in February of 1937. She would fly east to west, starting in Oakland, California. Amelia told reporters, "I think I have just one more long flight in my system." At one point, George told Amelia he thought the flight would get more publicity if she flew over the Pacific Ocean—a distance of 2,000 miles (3,200 km)—without a navigator. She said no to this dangerous plan.

"I think I have just one more long flight in my system."

*Honolulu, Hawaii, in 1937, left to right: Paul Mantz,
Amelia, Harry Manning, and Fred Noonan*

On March 17, 1937, Amelia and her crew took
off from Oakland and arrived in Oahu, Hawaii,
fifteen hours and forty-three minutes later. This
was a new speed record for the journey.

Mantz, who traveled with the crew for this
first leg of the trip, worked on one of the propel-
lers before allowing Amelia, Manning, and Noonan
to fly on. Then they had to wait until March 20 for

the weather to clear. On takeoff early that morning, the Electra, extremely heavy with fuel, spun on the ground on its belly, tearing away large pieces of the wing and its underside. No one is sure why this happened, but Harry Manning later said that Amelia's inexperience caused the crash. Amelia and George, as usual, blamed the accident on mechanical failure, though they were not sure exactly what had happened.

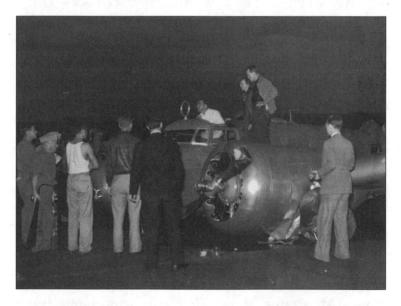

On March 20, 1937, the Electra crashed on takeoff from Hawaii. This photo shows the damage to a propeller and the underside of the plane. Atop the aircraft are (left to right) Paul Mantz, Amelia, and Fred Noonan.

The plane was shipped back to the Lockheed factory in California for repairs. George and Amelia immediately began looking for donations to pay for the work. It would be two months before the plane would be ready to fly again. Captain Manning was unable to continue on with the crew. He had to report back to his ship. Neither Amelia nor Noonan had as much experience in radio communications as Manning.

They had to reroute the trip to try to avoid spring storms. They would now reverse their course and fly west to east, starting in Miami, Florida. The change meant that all permissions from foreign governments and countless other details had to be done over. They did not inform the press of the change of plans until the very last minute.

ON HER WAY AROUND THE WORLD

Amelia and Fred Noonan left Miami on June 1, 1937. They left behind the telegraph key and the trailing communications antenna that had to be reeled in and out of the plane. Without them, they would be out of touch with homing signals for hours at a time. The telegraph would not have done them much good, anyway—neither Noonan nor Amelia had ever learned Morse code.

The first day, they flew to San Juan, Puerto

Rico. The trip was underway. But Amelia was getting tired of these long-distance flights. In *Last Flight,* she wrote about hurrying to leave San Juan: "We're always pushing through, hurrying on our long way, trying to get to some other place instead of enjoying the place we'd already got to."

But she did push through—east toward Africa. As they approached the coast of West Africa in a thick haze, Fred Noonan, sitting at his chart table in the back of the plane, figured out where they were and sent a note to Amelia in the front. It told her when to turn south to head for Dakar, their planned stop in western Africa. To get the note to her, he attached it to a line on a fishing pole they had rigged up. (It was too noisy in the plane to talk.) She read the note but believed Noonan had made an error. Her instinct told her to turn north, so she did, but they ended up in a town north of Dakar. Noonan had been right.

Then it was over to Karachi, India, south to Singapore, and across to Darwin, Australia. At each stop they rested, ate, and refueled and checked the plane. All along the way, Amelia was sending regular reports to George, who passed them along to newspaper reporters. All over the United States, anxious fans read her accounting of events in the newspaper.

They landed in Lae, New Guinea, on June 29. They had flown 22,000 miles (35,400 km) in one

ROUTE OF AMELIA EARHART'S ROUND-THE-WORLD FLIGHT

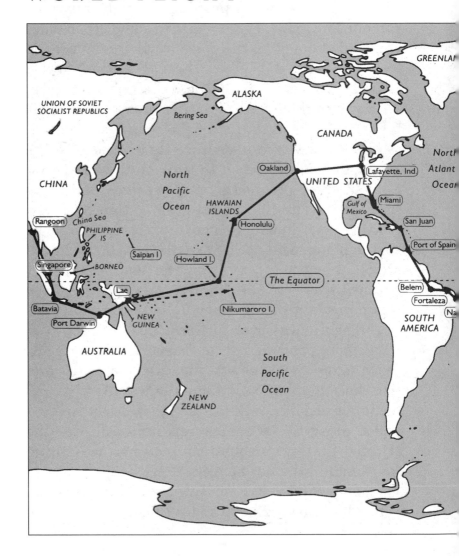

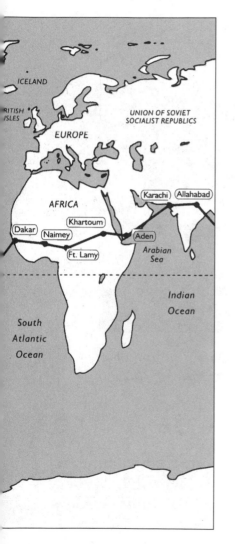

month, making thirty stops in nineteen countries on five continents. They were exhausted. In Lae, Amelia and Fred got some sleep while the plane was checked over and refueled. Noonan had been drinking heavily, and it bothered Amelia. Bad weather kept them there for three days. From Lae she wrote in her journal, "I wish we could stay here peacefully for a time and see something of this strange land." But they had only 7,000 miles (11,300 km) to go.

Before they took off, Amelia packed up maps, clothing, and other things they would not need and sent them back home. She wanted the plane to be as light as possible. She also took survival equipment off the plane, so concerned was she about extra weight.

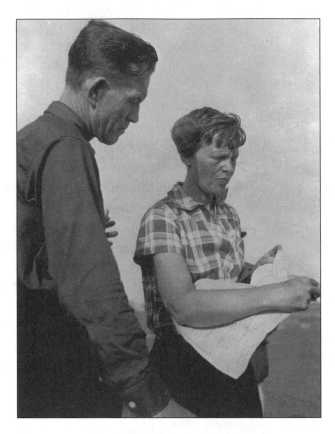

Fred Noonan and Amelia in Dakar, capital of what was then called French West Africa.

FROM LAE TO HOWLAND ISLAND

The weather cleared, and they took off on July 2, heading for tiny Howland Island in the Pacific Ocean. The U.S. Department of the Interior had built a runway there for the Electra. From

Howland, they were to fly to Hawaii, and from there to Oakland, California.

This was the most dangerous part of the trip. The airspace from Lae to Howland had never been mapped, and Howland would be hard to spot, even for the most experienced navigator. It was only two miles long and a half mile wide (3.2 by .8 km). Fred was expert at navigating by the stars, but this method would not work if the sky was cloudy. The U.S. Coast Guard provided a ship called the *Itasca*, stationed just off Howland Island, which would help guide the plane to the island. They would use black smoke signals and talk to the Electra on the radio.

The trip was expected to take about eighteen hours.

Radio operators were stationed on Howland Island and the *Itasca*. Amelia had said she would use frequency 3105 on the radio and report every half hour. The crew of the *Itasca* had a hard time hearing her. They asked her to switch to a stronger frequency but never received an answer. It seemed that she could not hear their requests.

They asked her several times to stay on the radio a few extra seconds so they could get a bearing on the plane. Each time, though, she signed off hurriedly.

At 4:53 A.M., a radioman on the *Itasca* thought he heard Amelia say "partly cloudy." There was a lot of static on the line. She said she would whistle into the microphone. She asked for a bearing on the plane, but she did not stay on the radio long enough to allow them to do this. She said she was 200 miles (320 km) out.

"We must be on you but cannot see you. Gas is running low."

The crew of the *Itasca* grew alarmed. It was obvious there was a problem with the plane's radio or with the way Amelia was using it. They repeatedly tried to reach her, but she never answered. When they finally did hear from her, it did little to put them at ease. "We must be on you but cannot see you. Gas is running low," she said. "Been unable to reach you by radio. Flying at 1,000 feet. Only half hour's gas left."

The *Itasca* began sending up thick black smoke signals. The sky was clear, and Amelia and Fred would surely have been able to see them if the plane was in the area.

At 8:47 A.M., Amelia's voice came in loud and clear, but hurried and panicked. "We are on line of position one five seven dash three three seven," Amelia said. "Will repeat this message on 6210 kilocycles. Wait, listening on 6210 kilocycles. We are running north and south."

The *Itasca* radioman responded immediately, asking her to stay on 3105 kilocycles. "Please stay on 3105 do not hear you on 6210," they said. But they did not hear from her again, on any frequency.

The U.S. Coast Guard ship Itasca *was to guide
Amelia to tiny Howland Island, shown here,
where an airstrip had been built for her landing.
The ship stayed on instead to help in the search
effort around the island.*

About an hour later, when the crew of the
Itasca calculated that the Electra would have
run out of fuel, a search party went out. Around
Howland Island, and to the south and east, the
weather was clear. To the north and west were
heavy cloud banks. The Electra must have been
in that area, they reasoned. This would explain
why the plane could not see the smoke signals. It

would also explain why Noonan had gotten so far off course, if he was not able to see the stars or the sun.

What followed was the largest sea search in the history of the U.S. Navy. As the days went on, a battleship, four destroyers, a minesweeper, a seaplane, and airplanes joined the search. They searched 25,000 square miles (65,000 sq km) of the Pacific. At first, the rescuers had high hopes of finding the fliers. Perhaps they were floating on a rubber raft or had been picked up by a Japanese fishing boat. Maybe the plane itself could float on its empty fuel tanks.

After many days of intense effort, however, the search teams found nothing.

CHAPTER SEVEN

WHAT HAPPENED TO AMELIA EARHART?

The search teams in the Pacific claimed that there was absolutely no trace of Amelia's plane. Or was there?

Did someone—the Japanese or the U.S. government—really know what happened to Amelia and Fred Noonan?

The disappearance of Amelia Earhart, Fred Noonan, and the Electra is one of the biggest mysteries of the twentieth century. The U.S. government's official position is that the plane ran out of gas shortly after the last time the *Itasca* heard from them, then it crashed at sea and sank. Many people do not believe this, however. For one thing, a plane that big would not have sunk right away. For another, the sunken plane would have left an oil or gas slick behind on the water. Nothing like this was ever found, despite the huge area of ocean they searched.

Many historians, aviation experts, reporters, and investigators have since tried to solve the puzzle. To date, no one knows for sure what happened. But here are some of the theories.

DID THEY SURVIVE THE CRASH?

For several days after the *Itasca* heard its last message from Amelia, a number of ham radio operators say they heard messages that they are sure came from the Electra. A Pan Am operator on Wake Island in the Pacific filed an official report stating that he had heard this message the day after the search began:

> SOS . . . SOS . . . SOS . . . SOS . . . Northwest unknown island 177 longitude . . . Quite down, but radio still working . . . Battery very weak . . . Don't know how long we can hold out . . . We are OK but a little wet . . . Calling [on] 3105 kilocycles . . . Give me a long call (fade out) KHAQQ [Amelia's call letters] . . . Plane on cay northwest Howland Island . . . Both OK. One wing broken. Bearing 337 . . . 58 minutes above equator L.A.T. Island 133 acres . . . Must be a new one.

Another operator, forty years after the incident, reported that he had heard Amelia say they had crashed and were floating in the sea. He was only fifteen at the time of the flight and did not think anyone would believe him. He said that as he listened, the woman's voice became frightened and that Japanese soldiers were beating Fred Noonan; she cried out, asking them not to hurt her. Then the transmission went dead.

Can we believe any of these reports? Were the transmissions fake? Perhaps there were other radio operators pretending to be Amelia as part of a cruel hoax? Or were the broadcasts real, and some people did not want the truth to come out?

WERE THEY SPIES?

One theory is that Amelia Earhart was spying for the U.S. government. Some people believe that her airplane was specially equipped with cameras to take pictures in the Pacific. At the time of the flight, the U.S. government believed the Japanese were getting ready to enter into warfare. (It was shortly before the start of World War II.) The government wanted to get evidence that the Japanese were building military bases in the Pacific, something they were not supposed to do.

Many things about Amelia's last flight do not add up. Why didn't she ever stay on the radio long enough to allow the *Itasca* to get her position? And why did she keep changing frequencies? There are three possible answers: one, she was an inexperienced radio operator; two, she did not want Japanese ships, which she knew were in the area, to know where she was; or three, she did not want the *Itasca* to know where she was because she was actually flying off course on purpose and spying for the U.S. government.

There are more questions. Why, for example, did she leave some of her radio equipment behind in Miami? Why did she switch course—from east-to-west to west-to-east—at the last minute? She ended up flying through many spring storms, though she said she had reversed the course to avoid them. Why did the government build a runway especially for Amelia at Howland Island? And why the huge and expensive search effort for two civilians? Other fliers had not received such attention.

At least one investigator believes that after Amelia wrecked the Electra on takeoff in Honolulu, the U.S. government approached her about spying. When the plane was grounded after the crash, the team needed money for repairs in order to go on with the flight. According to this spy theory, instead of rebuilding the plane, they constructed a whole new Electra, a much faster and more powerful model, with cameras installed in the belly. It looked enough like the original to pass. The government could have had the ability to conduct such an operation—after all, Amelia and George were good friends with President Roosevelt himself. This theory would mean that all the calculations about the plane's location could be wrong because the new plane might have been able to go faster than people thought. This would explain why Amelia and Fred were not found in the search area—maybe they had flown out of it.

Whether the fliers were spying or not, the Japanese would have been suspicious of any plane flying over their territory. If a plane had gone down near them, they would have investigated the crash. It is quite possible that they would have taken Amelia and Fred prisoner. The Japanese did not let the U.S. search party into their waters, or onto the islands they controlled, to look for Amelia and Fred.

WAS AMELIA STILL ALIVE?

In the early 1960s, U.S. Air Force Major Joe Gervais went to Saipan, an island some 2,660 miles (4,280 km) north of Howland. Saipan was an important military base for the Japanese during the war and had a military prison. Gervais had heard rumors that Fred and Amelia had been taken to Saipan, and he interviewed many people about the possibility. A short time later, Fred Goerner, a CBS reporter, also traveled to the island to interview residents who said they had seen the two.

Some evidence suggests that Amelia and Fred Noonan were held on the island of Saipan. This photo shows an old Japanese prison on the island, where it is rumored the two were held briefly by the Japanese.

More than one hundred of the island's natives who were living there in the time just before World War II said the same thing: they were sure the two were Amelia and Fred. When Goerner showed the islanders photographs of several women, all of them picked Amelia as the woman they had seen.

Some say that Amelia died of a disease called dysentery, and that Fred was shot by the Japanese when he made them mad. Others say they were both executed.

Many searches were made of the island, and in one search, some bones from two skeletons were found. When the bones were analyzed, however, it turned out they were not the remains of Fred and Amelia. Aside from the testimony of the residents of the island, no hard evidence could be found that Fred and Amelia were held on Saipan. A hot trail had gone cold.

Amelia's family did not give up the hope that Amelia was still alive. Some people suggested that Amelia had been brainwashed and was "Tokyo Rose," a woman who read propaganda reports over the radio meant to confuse American military personnel during World War II. George traveled to Japan to hear her; he denied the woman's voice was Amelia's. Fourteen months after Amelia disappeared, George had her declared legally dead, and he married another woman a short time later.

Amelia's mother and sister hoped that Amelia might return home after the war ended. They would be bitterly disappointed. Amy believed Amelia had left a large estate and fought with George over her will. She never wanted to admit that her daughter wasn't coming back and kept up hope until she died, at age ninety-five, in 1967. Muriel, who also had hopes of seeing her sister again, continued living in Massachusetts, lecturing and writing two books about Amelia; she was ninety-seven years old in 1997. Muriel believes that Amelia was "a tragedy of the sea."

Several years ago, a writer digging through government documents on Amelia found a telegram. It was from China, addressed to George Palmer Putnam in California. The date of the telegram was August 28, 1945, after the liberation of a prison camp in China. It said, "Camp liberated; all well. Volumes to tell. Love to mother." Whether that telegram was really from Amelia or not, we do not know.

Another theory, which few people believe, is that Amelia survived the war, was released from prison camp afterward, and returned to the United States under a different name. Joe Gervais, who investigated a mystery woman named Irene Bolam, makes an interesting case. The woman lived in a house belonging to Amelia's good friend Jacqueline Cochran. The woman was also a pilot and a member of the Ninety-Nines and Zonta International, two flying groups to which Amelia belonged. When Gervais looked into their records, however, he found no Irene Bolam in their registers. She told him that she had been licensed under a different name. Still, she strongly denied that she was Amelia Earhart, and she sued author Joe Klaas to stop him from publishing a book that described Gervais's findings.

THE SEARCH CONTINUES

We may never know for sure what became of Amelia and Fred and the Electra, but the search for the plane and clues continues. As I write this book, a team of researchers is searching an island called Nikumaroro, southeast of Howland. It was called Gardner Island in the 1940s. Many artifacts have been found there, including parts from a plane, but no one is sure they came from Amelia's Electra.

Though nothing has yet been confirmed, two compelling discoveries have been made at Nikumaroro: the remains of a shoe that was Amelia's size and a piece of metal that has been analyzed and found to be the same type of metal that Amelia's Electra was made of. The International Group for Historic Aircraft Recovery (TIGHAR), the team that searched the island, says that the U.S. government first searched Nikumaroro in the 1940s but did not go very far into it. TIGHAR reasons that Fred and Amelia may have taxied the plane into a cooler area under trees, where it would not have been seen by the search planes overhead.

Fliers Elgen and Marie Long of California, along with a man named Roy Nesbit, believe the Electra probably ran out of gas and plunged into

Researchers found these artifacts on the island of Nikumaroro. The large piece of aircraft skin in the center is made of the same material as the Electra. Also found was the sole of a woman's shoe (top left) that could have belonged to Amelia.

the ocean about 40 miles (64 km) northwest of Howland Island. Nesbit, relying on records from Lae, found that Amelia did not take off with a full tank of gas and only had enough to make it to

Howland under perfect conditions. The Longs have established a fund to conduct the expensive search of the deep ocean bed. Only parts of the plane would still be intact today, but the mystery would be solved.

The controversy surrounding the plane's disappearance has captured the interest of countless people ever since that day in 1937. But did Amelia's last flight mean anything? Did it advance the cause of aviation or of women fliers, as she said she wanted it to? Yes. On a practical level, Amelia's flight led to new emergency procedures for fliers. For the future of aviation, people across the world could see that a plane was able to fly 22,000 miles (35,400 km) and more.

On another level, Amelia showed people that sometimes life is about taking risks, about proving things to yourself. She showed the world that women are risk-takers, too. Above all, she served as an inspiration to girls—and boys—everywhere. She lived her life exactly the way she wanted to, no matter what other people thought. In some ways, she always remained the girl in brown who walked alone. She spoke out about things that bothered her, and she fought for things she believed in. She was one of the true independent spirits of the twentieth century.

It is sad that Amelia did not live to see the

day when people would fly places almost as easily as they board a bus, to see the day when millions of young girls would be able to gaze out of an airplane window and see the night sky Amelia loved so much and dream of the things they might accomplish.

This is believed to be the last photograph taken of Amelia Earhart. She posed with a man named Jacobs (center) and Fred Noonan just before takeoff from Lae on July 2, 1937.

CHRONOLOGY

1897	Born in Atchison, Kansas, on July 24.
1899	Sister, Muriel, born on December 29.
1903	Orville and Wilbur Wright make their first flight.
1907	Edwin and Amy Earhart move to Des Moines, Iowa.
1908	Moves to Des Moines; sees first airplane and is not impressed.
1912	Amelia, Muriel, and Amy Earhart move to Hyde Park, Illinois.
1917	The United States enters World War I.
1918	Becomes Red Cross nurse's aide.
1920	Joins parents in California; meets Sam Chapman; takes flying lessons from Neta Snook.
1922	Buys the *Canary,* her first plane; sets women's altitude record.
1924	Edwin and Amy Earhart file for divorce.
1926	Amy and Amelia join Muriel in Massachusetts; Amelia begins work in Denison House.

1927	Charles Lindbergh makes first solo flight across Atlantic Ocean; Amelia asked to cross the Atlantic in the *Friendship*.
1928	Becomes first woman to cross the Atlantic by air; stays at house of George Palmer ("G. P.") Putnam to write *20 hrs. 40 min.*
1929	The Ninety-Nines holds first meeting, elects Amelia its first president.
1930	Dorothy Putnam files for divorce from G. P. Putnam.
1931	Marries G. P. Putnam on February 7; sets two altitude records for autogiro, becomes first woman to pilot one across the United States.
1932	Becomes first woman to cross the Atlantic solo; takes Eleanor Roosevelt up in plane.
1935	Becomes first person to fly from Hawaii to U.S. mainland, first person to solo from Los Angeles to Mexico City, and first person to solo from Mexico City to Newark, New Jersey; joins faculty of Purdue University in Lafayette, Indiana.
1936	Receives Lockheed Electra airplane from Purdue Research Foundation.
1937	Begins first attempt to fly around the world with flight from Oakland, California, to Honolulu, Hawaii, in March, but crashes plane on takeoff from Honolulu; leaves Miami on June 1 in second attempt at round-the-world flight; takes off from Lae, New Guinea, on July 2, disappears over Pacific Ocean.

MAJOR AVIATION RECORDS SET BY AMELIA EARHART

October 1922: Women's altitude record, 14,000 feet (4,270 m)

June 1928: First woman to cross the Atlantic by air

July 1930: Speed records for 100 kilometers and for 100 kilometers with freight of 500 pounds (230 kg)

April 1931: Altitude record for autogiros, 15,000 feet (4,572 m)
New altitude record for autogiros, 18,415 feet (5,613 m)
First woman to pilot an autogiro across the United States

May 1932: First woman to cross the Atlantic solo
First person to cross the Atlantic twice
Longest nonstop flight by a woman, 2,026 miles (3,260 km)

August 1932: Speed record for women's nonstop transcontinental flight—Los Angeles, California, to Newark, New Jersey, in 19 hours, 15 minutes

July 1933: New record for transcontinental travel, breaking own existing record, 17 hours, 7 minutes

January 1935: First person to fly from Honolulu, Hawaii, to Oakland, California, 2,408 miles (3,875 km) in 17 hours, 7 minutes
First person to solo anywhere in the Pacific
First person to solo over both the Atlantic and Pacific Oceans

April 1935: First person to solo from Los Angeles to Mexico City, 13 hours, 23 minutes

May 1935: First person to solo from Mexico City to Newark, New Jersey, 14 hours, 19 minutes

March 1937: Record for east-to-west crossing—Oakland, California, to Honolulu in 15 hours, 43 minutes

June–July 1937: First person to attempt to fly around the globe at the equator—22,000 miles (35,400 km) flown

SOURCES

Chapter 1

Amelia Earhart, *The Fun of It* (Academy Chicago Publishers, Chicago, 1992).

Mary S. Lovell, *The Sound of Wings* (St. Martin's Press, New York, 1989).

Muriel Morrissey, *Courage Is the Price* (McCormick-Armstrong, Wichita, Kans., 1963).

Chapter 2

Amelia Earhart, *The Fun of It* (Academy Chicago Publishers, Chicago, 1992).

Muriel Morrissey, *Courage Is the Price* (McCormick-Armstrong, Wichita, Kans., 1963).

Neta Snook Southern, *I Taught Amelia to Fly* (Vantage Press, New York, 1974).

Chapter 3

Amelia Earhart, *The Fun of It* (Academy Chicago Publishers, Chicago, 1992).

Amelia Earhart, *20 hrs. 40 min.* (G. P. Putnam's Sons, New York, 1929).

Muriel Morrissey, *Courage Is the Price* (McCormick-Armstrong, Wichita, Kans., 1963).

Chapter 4

Mary S. Lovell, *The Sound of Wings* (St. Martin's Press, New York, 1989).

George Palmer Putnam, *Soaring Wings* (Harcourt, Brace, New York, 1939); Amelia's marriage "contract" is reprinted from this source.

Chapter 5

Jean L. Backus, *Letters from Amelia* (Beacon Press, Boston, 1982).

Mary S. Lovell, *The Sound of Wings* (St. Martin's Press, New York, 1989).

Chapter 6

Amelia Earhart, *Last Flight* (1937; reprint, Crown, New York, 1988).

Mary S. Lovell, *The Sound of Wings* (St. Martin's Press, New York, 1989).

Chapter 7

Randall Brink, *Lost Star* (W. W. Norton, New York, 1994).

Fred Goerner, *The Search for Amelia Earhart* (Doubleday, New York, 1966).

Muriel Morrissey, *Courage Is the Price* (McCormick-Armstrong, Wichita, Kans., 1963).

TIGHAR Tracks, a publication of The International Group for Historic Aircraft Recovery (September 30, 1996).

FOR MORE INFORMATION

Backus, Jean L. *Letters from Amelia*. Boston: Beacon Press, 1982.

Brink, Randall. *Lost Star*. New York: W.W. Norton & Company, 1994.

Earhart, Amelia. *The Fun of It*. Chicago: Academy Chicago Publishers, 1992.

———. *Last Flight*. 1937. Reprint, New York: Crown, 1988.

———. *20 hrs. 40 min*. New York: G.P. Putnam's Sons, 1929.

Goerner, Fred. *The Search for Amelia Earhart*. New York: Doubleday, 1966.

Lovell, Mary S. *The Sound of Wings*. New York: St. Martin's Press, 1989.

Putnam, George Palmer. *Soaring Wings*. New York: Harcourt, Brace and Company, 1939.

Southern, Neta Snook. *I Taught Amelia to Fly*. New York: Vantage Press, 1974.

Movie

Flight for Freedom (1943) starring Rosalind Russell and Fred MacMurray. This was the movie that led many to believe Amelia Earhart was on a spy mission for the U.S. government.

Internet Resources

Due to the changeable nature of the Internet, sites appear and disappear very quickly. Internet addresses must be entered exactly as they appear.

The Yahoo directory of the World Wide Web is an excellent place to find Internet sites on any topic. The directory is located at:

http://www.yahoo.com

The official Web site of Amelia Earhart from CMG Worldwide contains quotations, photographs, career highlights, and information on Linda Finch's planned flight:

http://www.cmgww.com/historic/earhart/

Linda Finch is a businesswoman from Texas who has taken a Lockheed Electra plane identical to Earhart's on a journey recreating the flight around the world. Pratt & Whitney, sponsor of the endeavor, is maintaining a site for following the preparation and progress of the flight:

http://www.worldflight.org

The "Earhart Project" is an investigation conducted by The International Group for Historic Aircraft Recovery (TIGHAR) to solve the mystery of Amelia Earhart's disappearance:

http://www.tighar.org/Projects/AEdescr.html

INDEX

Numbers in *italics* represent illustrations.

Airshow, 35–36
Atlantic solo flight, 59–74
Autogiro, 54–57, *55*

Balchen, Bernt, 60
Beech Nut Packing Company, 55
Black Beauty (Sewell), 16
Bolam, Irene, 96
Byrd, Admiral Richard, 40, 44

Canary (plane), 33–37
Chapman, Sam, 28–29, 32, 36–37, 38
Cochran, Jacqueline, 96
Columbia University, 27, 37
Curtiss Canuck (plane), 30, *31*, 33

Dakar, 81, *84*

Daughters of the American Revolution, 68
Denison House, 37–39, 48
Douglas, Donald, 33

Earhart, Amelia, 9–10, *14, 17, 61, 78, 79, 100*
    called "Lady Lindy," 45
    celebrity of, 64
    disappearance of, 7–10, 85–88, 89–100
    education of, 13, 15–16, 20–21, 27, 37
    and feminism, 68, 76
    first crash of, 33–34
    first jobs of, 30, 32
    flying lessons of, 28–34, *31*
    flying records of, 54, 63–64, 67, 75, 78
    last flight of, 7–8, 75–88
    as lecturer, 65, 68, 72
    marriage to George Putnam, 27, 49–58, *50*

as model, 47, *48*
at Purdue, 73–74
search for, 89–100
theories about disap-
  pearance of, 90–93
transatlantic   flight
  aboard   *Friendship*,
  39–47, *43, 46*
as volunteer, 24–26, *25*
Earhart, Amy Otis (mother),
  11–21, 28, 36–38, 65–67,
  95
Earhart,   Edwin   (father),
  11–21, 28, 37, 52
  alcoholism of, 16–17, 77
Earhart, Muriel (sister), 12,
  17, 24, 25, 28, 37–38,
  65–67, 95–96

Feminism, 68, 76
Fokker F7 (plane), 40–42
Friendship flight, 35–48, *43*

Gallagher's pasture, 62–63
Gervais, Joe, 93–94, 96
Goerner, Fred, 93–94
Gordon, Lou, *46*
Gorski, Eddie, 60
Grosvener, Gilbert, *66*
Guest, Amy Phipps, 40

Hawaii flight, 69–72
  criticism of, 70
Hoover,   Herbert   and   Lou
  Henry, 65, *66*
Howland   (island),   7–10,
  84–88, *87*, 99

Industrial Workers of the
  World, 29
Itasca (ship), 8, 85–88, *87*

Japanese   military   bases,
  91–93

Kingsford-Smith,   Charles,
  70
Kinner Airster (*Canary*), 33,
  36, 37
Kissel (car), 37
Klass, Joe, 96

Lae, New Guinea, 81–85
LaGorce, John, *66*
Last Flight (Earhart), 75, 81
Last flight, 75–88
Lindbergh, Charles, 39
Lockheed   Electra   (plane),
  7–10, 74, *74*, 76, 84–85
  crash   on   takeoff   from
    Honolulu, 79, *79*
  search for, 89–100
Lockheed   Vega   (plane),
  59–64, *61*
Long,   Elgen   and   Marie,
  97–99

Manning, Harry, 77–79, *78*,
  79
Mantz, Paul, 69–70, 73, 76,
  78, 79
Map of last flight, 82–83
McDonnell Douglas, 33
Mexico City flight, 72
Montijo, John "Monte", 34

National Aeronautics Association, 38–39
National Women's Party, 68
Nesbit, Roy, 97–99
Nichols, Ruth, 36, 64
Nikumaroro (island), 97–98
Ninety-Nines, 68–69, 96
Noonan, Fred, 7–10, 77, *78, 79*, 80–88, *84, 100*
    alcoholism of, 77, 83
    search for, 89–100

Ogontz School, 22–26
Otis, Judge Alfred G., 12, 19
Otis, Amy, *See* Earhart, Amy Otis

Pan Am (airline), 77
Perkins, Marion, 41
Purdue University, 10, 73–74
Putnam, George, 40–41, 45, 47, *66*, 68, 77, 81, 95
    marriage to Amelia, 49–58, *50*

Railey, H. H., 39–40
Red Cross, 24, 26

Roosevelt, Eleanor, 71, 76
    flies with Amelia, 68
Roosevelt, Franklin D., 68, *71*, 76, 92–93

Saipan, (island), 93–95, *94*
Skyward (Byrd), 44
Snook, Anita "Neta", 30–35, *31*
Spirit of St. Louis, 39
Stultz, Bill, *46*, 47

TIGHAR (The International Group for Historic Aircraft Recovery), 97
"Tokyo Rose," 95
20 hrs. 40 min (Earhart), 47

Vega (Lockheed), 69–74

Women's rights, 10, 23, 68
World War I, 23
Wright, Orville and Wilbur, 18

Zonta International, 96

ABOUT THE AUTHOR

Jan Parr is a writer and editor living in Oak Park, Illinois. A graduate of the University of Missouri and the University of Iowa, she has published her work in many regional and national magazines. She is the author of *The Young Vegetarian's Companion* (Franklin Watts, 1996).